CONTENTS

Introduction 4

About the Video 5

Critical Acclaim 5

Chapter 1: Blues Chops 6

Chapter 2: Jazz Chops 31

Chapter 3: Rock Chops 51

Chapter 4: Fusion Chops 72

Chapter 5: R&B Chops 90

Chapter 6: Slapping Chops 114

About the Author 134

Bass Notation Legend 135

INTRODUCTION

The purpose of this book is to help you develop extraordinary technique on the bass guitar. While all my books focus on building various types of bass technique, I felt this book was necessary for several reasons. First, the scope of most of my other books, generally, is contained within a single style or skill (rock, blues, slapping, etc.). *Bass Chops* covers a cross section of musical genres with a unique, step-by-step approach for strengthening your overall facility on the instrument.

If you're familiar with my books, you know I'm a huge proponent of making everything groove, rather than just going through the motions of scales for scales' sake, or technique for technique's sake. As is my custom, each lesson is designed not only as an exercise, but as a musical composition *that grooves*.

In a sense, *Bass Chops* is a follow-up to my *Bass Aerobics* book, which was also designed for building bass technique. The two books, however, are quite different. While *Bass Aerobics* concentrates on a series of specific bass techniques (such as chromatics, scales/arpeggios, string crossings), each chapter in *Bass Chops* is centered around a specific genre of music (jazz, fusion, R&B, etc.), with every lesson jam packed with tons of chops-building bass lines and grooves. I've often described *Bass Aerobics* as a collection of "exercises that groove," or "grooves that are good for you." The same can be said about *Bass Chops*, but here we're going to take your bass playing to a whole new level.

The lessons in *Bass Chops* are structured around a *theme and variations* concept. Each lesson begins with a simple groove, which gradually becomes more intricate and more complex as the lesson progresses. You can move through each lesson at your own pace, taking on whichever examples are appropriate for your level of playing. As you become proficient with earlier portions in each lesson, you can move up to the more challenging material as your bass playing improves. This is the same approach I take with my online lessons. It has shown itself to be a highly effective approach to learning bass, and has become very popular with my students.

Remember, your primary role as a bass player is to lay down the groove and make the music feel good. Having great bass technique can be a powerful tool, giving you the ability to enhance the music significantly. Just be sure to use it tastefully and responsibly, lest you get fired for showing off "up there" when you should be playing the groove "down here."

I've provided fingerings, tablature, and video demonstrations, all of which I think you'll find helpful. (For the "Slapping Chops" chapter, a few special notation symbols are used; see the back of the book for details.) Some of the material gets mighty difficult, but don't let that intimidate you. I mean, hey, if you could already play everything here, you wouldn't need this book! Just take it one step at a time. By the time you get through *Bass Chops*, you'll be an amazing bass player. Congratulations and good luck!

– J.L.

BASS CHOPS

A step-by-step method for developing extraordinary technique on the bass guitar

BY JON LIEBMAN

Bass tracks and drum programming: Jon Liebman
Guitar: Adam Liebman

To access video visit:
www.halleonard.com/mylibrary

Enter Code
3651-7326-1903-0417

ISBN 978-1-5400-3652-0

Visit Hal Leonard Online at
www.halleonard.com

Contact us:
Hal Leonard
7777 West Bluemound Road
Milwaukee, WI 53213
Email: info@halleonard.com

In Europe, contact:
Hal Leonard Europe Limited
Distribution Centre, Newmarket Road
Bury St Edmunds, Suffolk, IP33 3YB
Email: info@halleonardeurope.com

In Australia, contact:
Hal Leonard Australia Pty. Ltd.
4 Lentara Court
Cheltenham, Victoria, 3192 Australia
Email: info@halleonard.com.au

ABOUT THE VIDEO

The video demonstrations that accompany this book are available online at *www.halleonard.com/mylibrary*. To access them for download or streaming, simply enter the code found on page 1 of this book.

In the book, repeat signs are shown for many of the playing examples, and you are encouraged to follow them as you practice. However, on the video demonstrations, the repeats are not played.

CRITICAL ACCLAIM

*"BASS CHOP*S is a great tool to get a strong, solid foundation as a bass player. Go get it now!"

—**Hadrien Feraud** (John McLaughlin, Lee Ritenour, Billy Cobham)

"BASS CHOPS is a phenomenal book—a must-have for anyone looking to develop some truly serious technique on the bass. Highly recommended!"

—**Bill "The Buddha" Dickens** (Aretha Franklin, Janet Jackson, Rope-A-Dope recording artist)

"Great exercises, and good practice for sight reading as well."

—**Bunny Brunel** (Chick Corea, Herbie Hancock, Wayne Shorter, Dizzy Gillespie)

"The new book by Jon Liebman, *BASS CHOPS*, gives you a program that will help develop your overall technique, while opening your mind to countless creative options for composing new basslines."

—**Freekbass** (Bootsy Collins, Buckethead, Bernie Worrell)

"BASS CHOPS continues Jon Liebman's tradition of creating useful progressive concepts and exercises for aspiring bassists looking to improve their foundation. A great introduction to a diverse collection of styles and phrases that can help players to build their technique, phrasing, reading, and timekeeping accuracy. Highly recommended!"

—**Adam Nitti** (Kenny Loggins, Carrie Underwood, Michael McDonald)

"Excellent for improving your reading while becoming well versed in blues, jazz, and rock bass lines!"

—**Brad Russell** (Joe Satriani, Gregg Bissonette, Rick Derringer)

Chapter 1: Blues Chops

BLUES 1

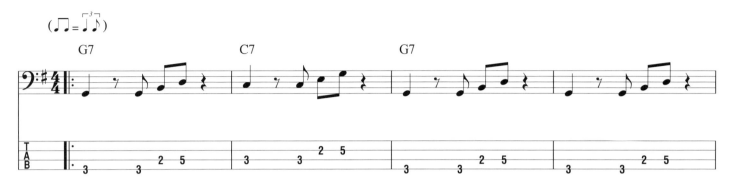

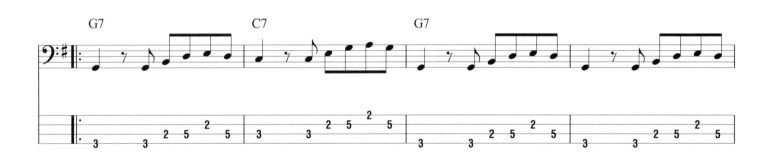

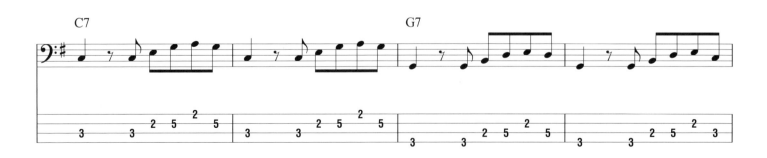

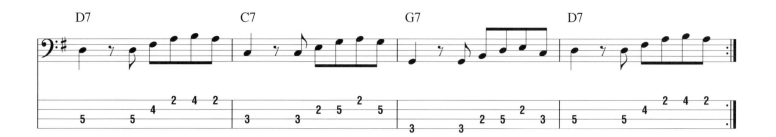

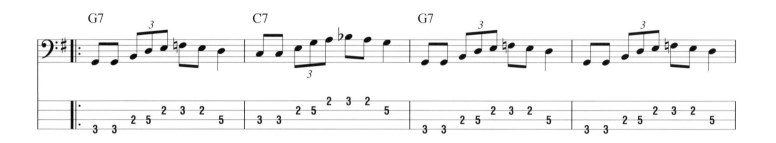

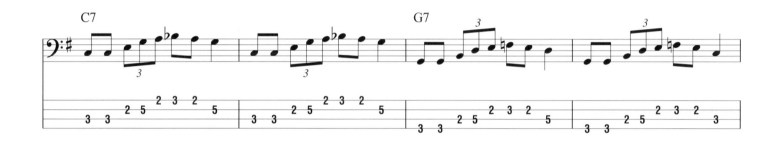

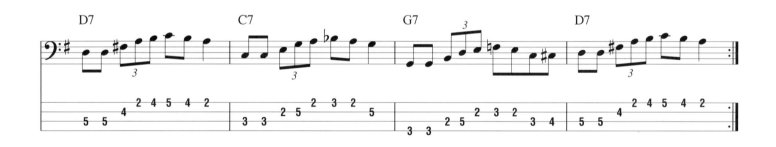

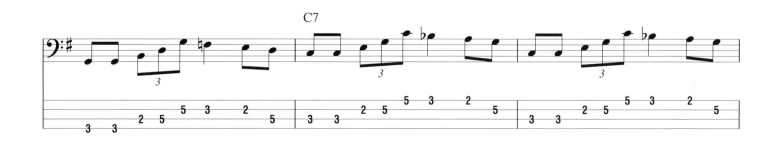

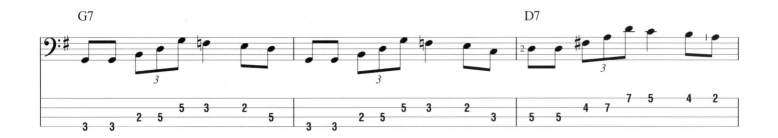

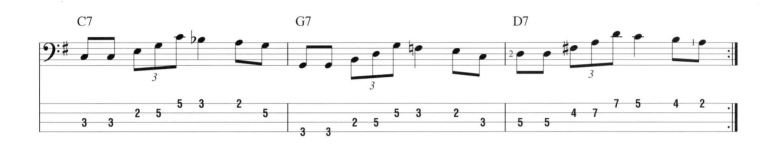

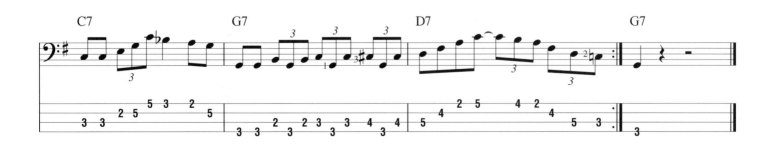

BLUES 2

11

BLUES 3

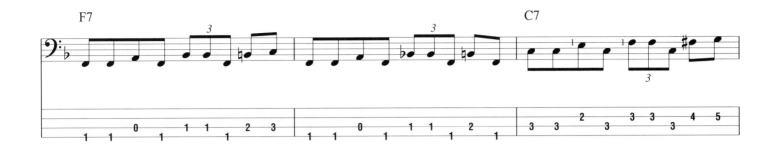

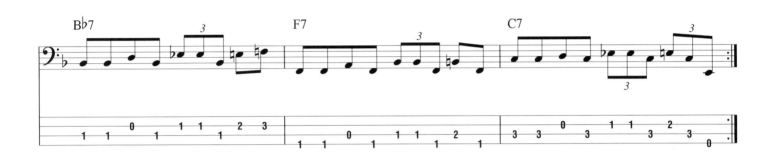

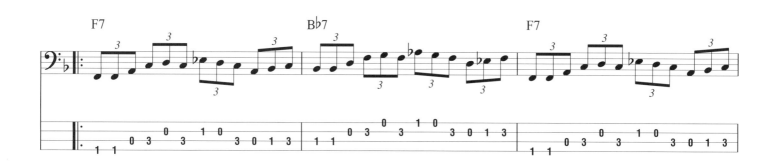

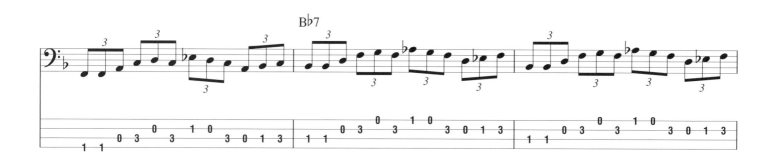

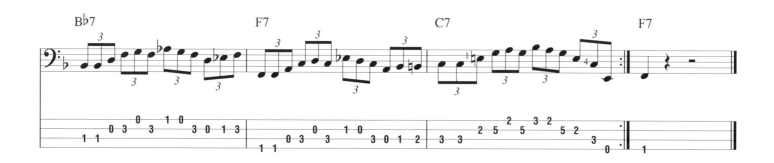

BLUES 4

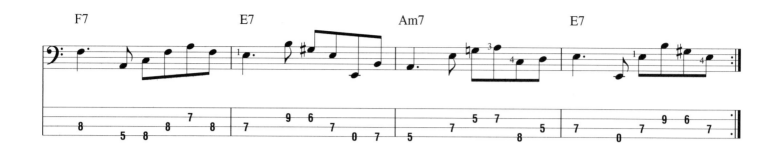

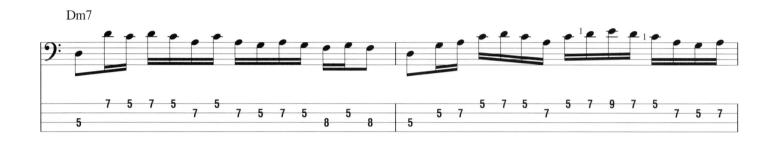

Dm7

Am7

F7   E7

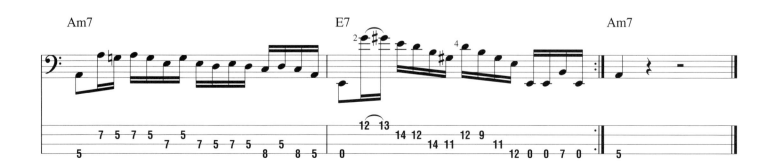

Am7   E7   Am7

BLUES 5

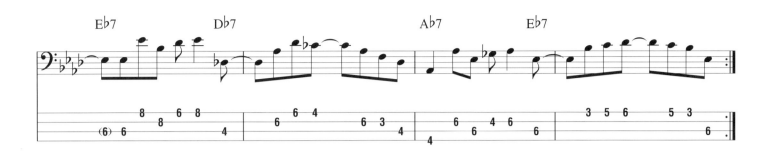

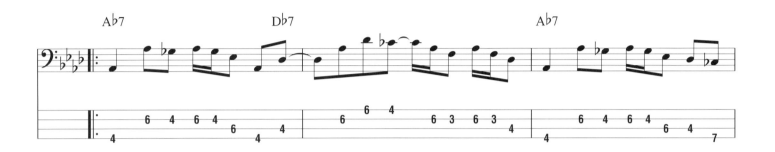

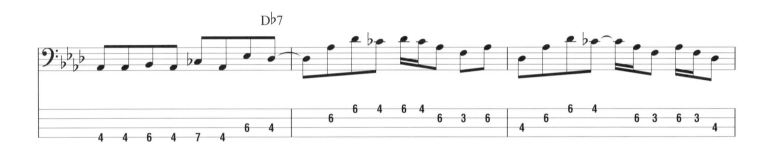

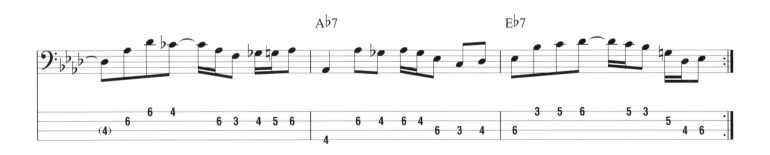

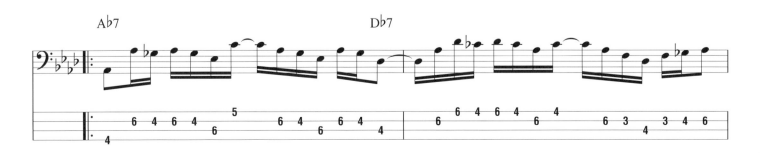

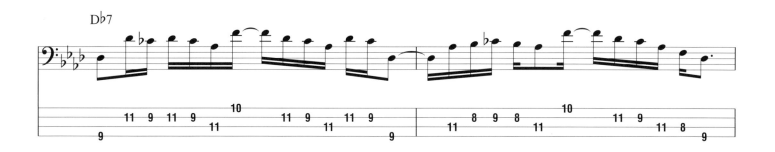

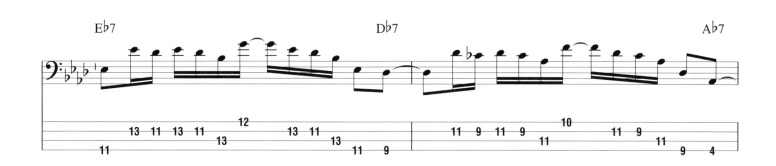

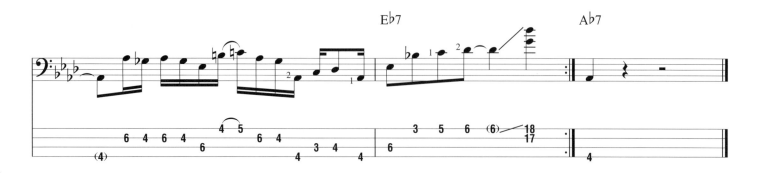

BLUES 6

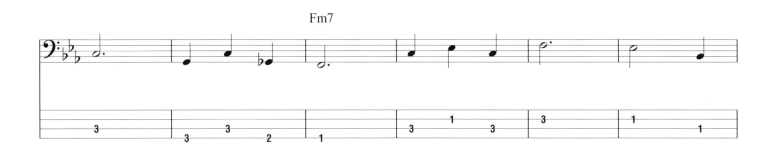

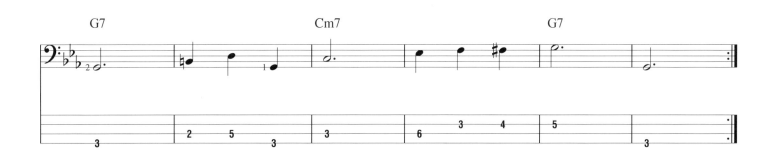

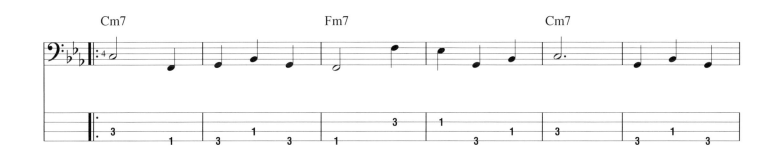

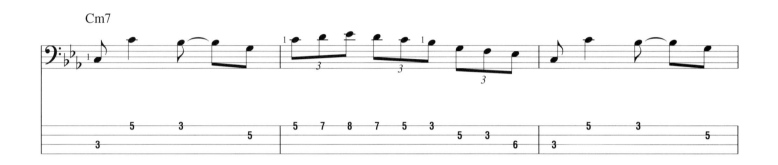

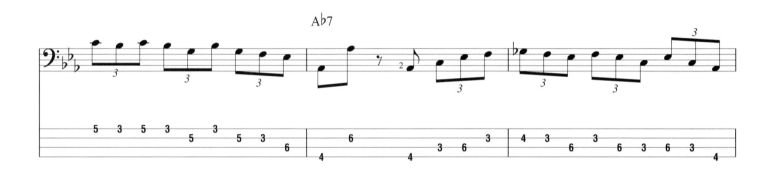

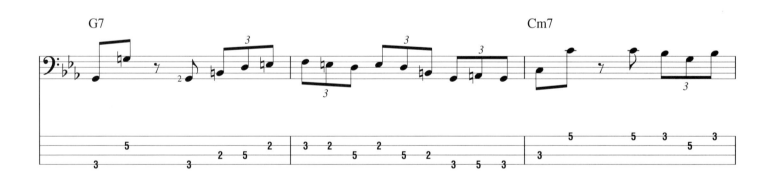

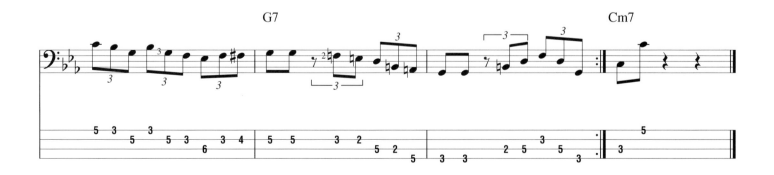

BLUES 7

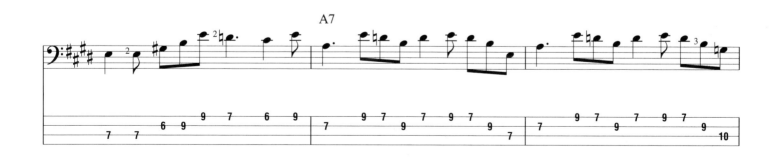

BLUES 8

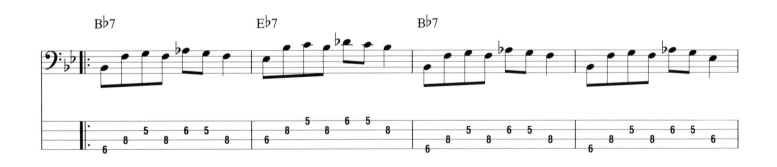

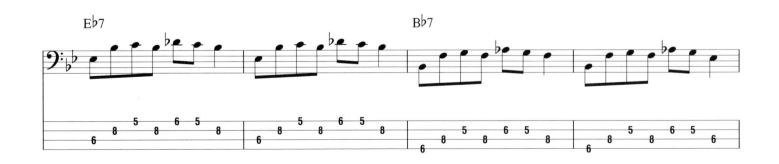

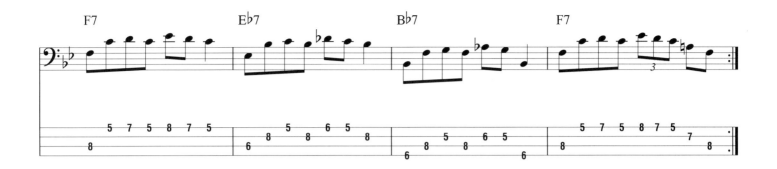

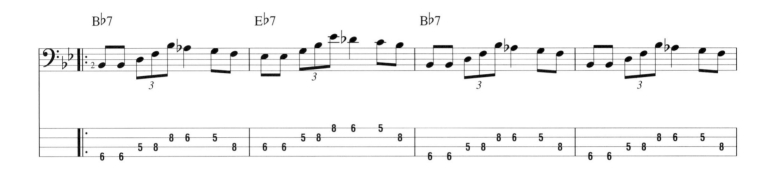

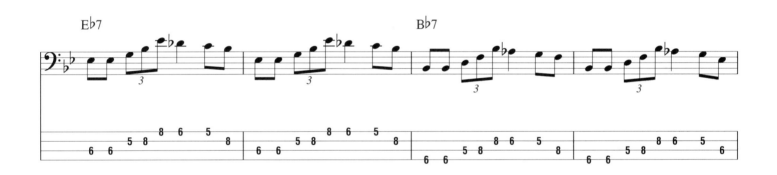

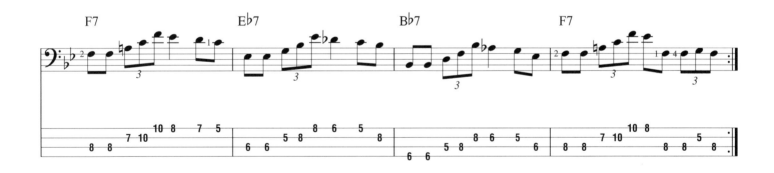

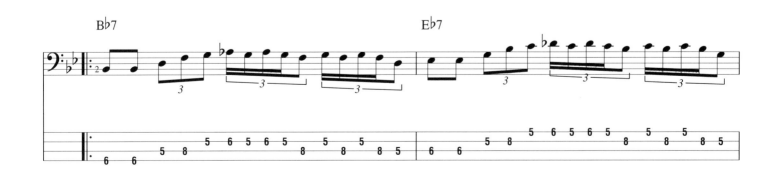

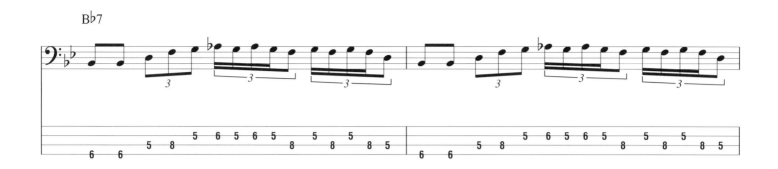

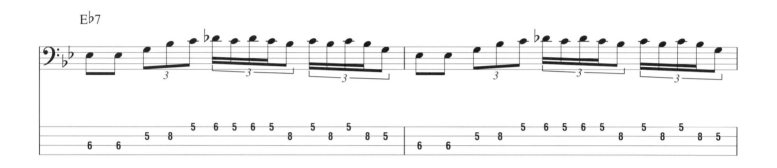

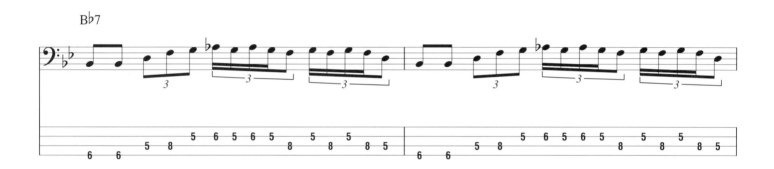

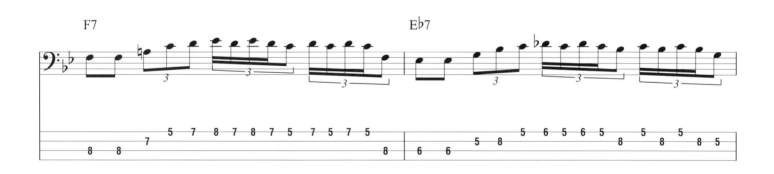

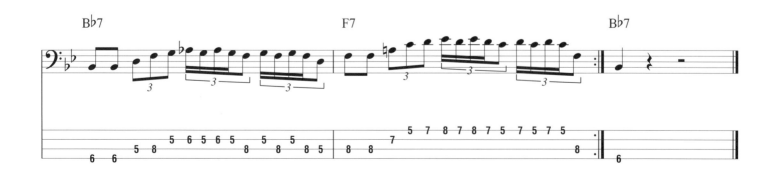

Chapter 2: Jazz Chops

JAZZ 1

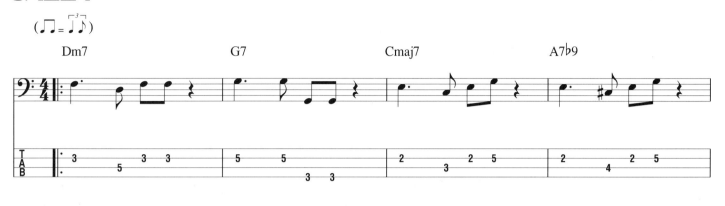

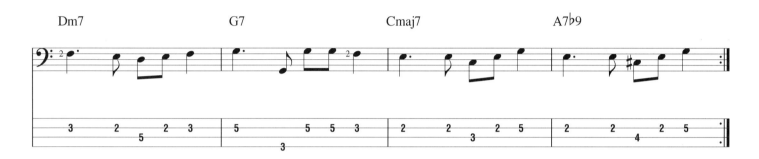

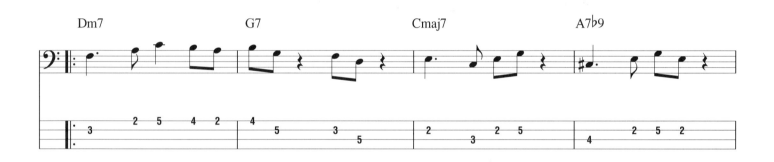

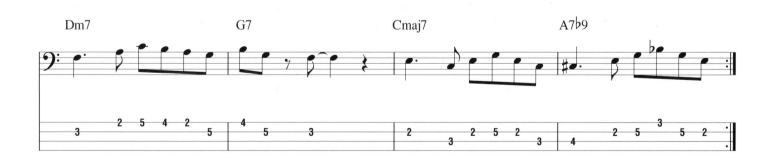

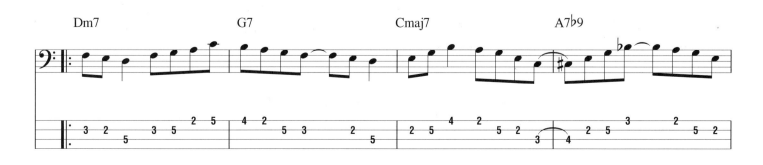

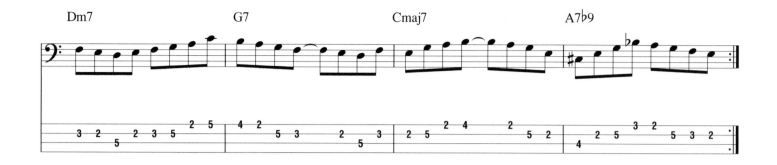

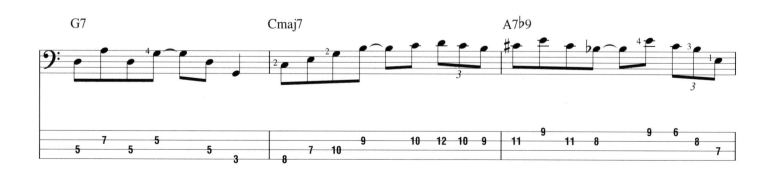

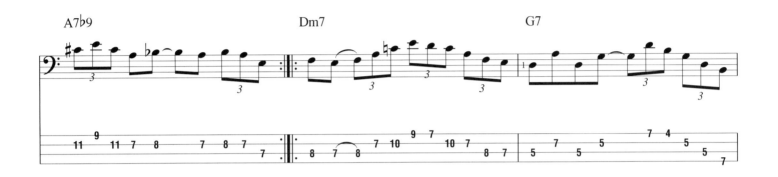

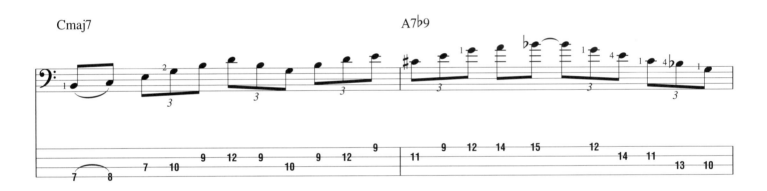

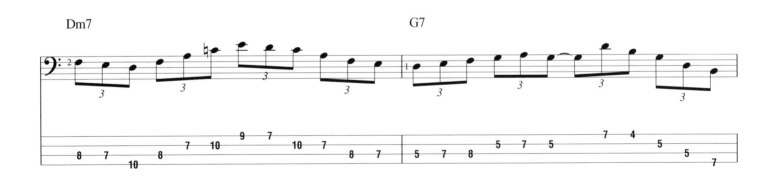

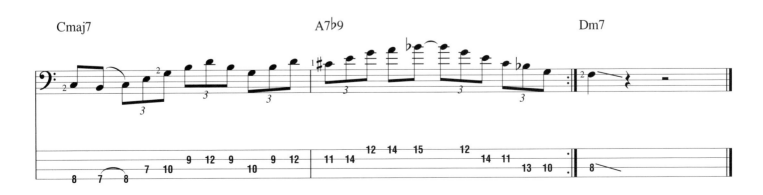

JAZZ 2

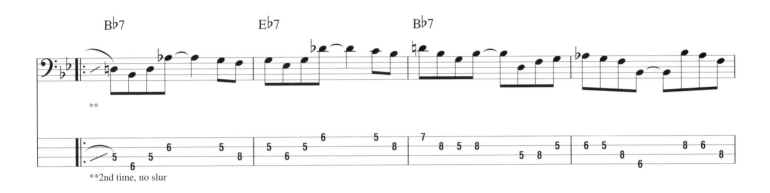

*1st time, no slur

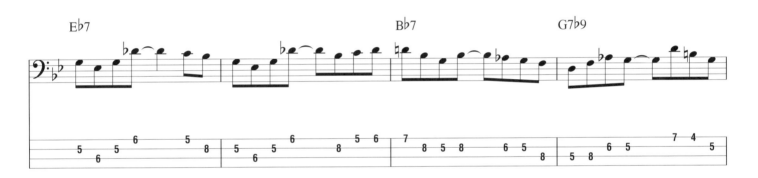

**2nd time, no slur

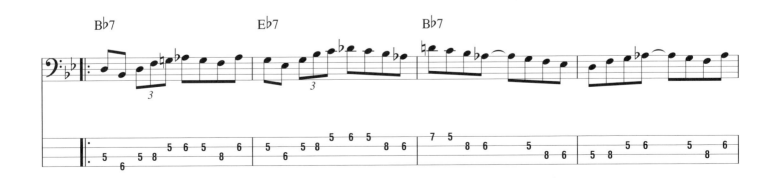

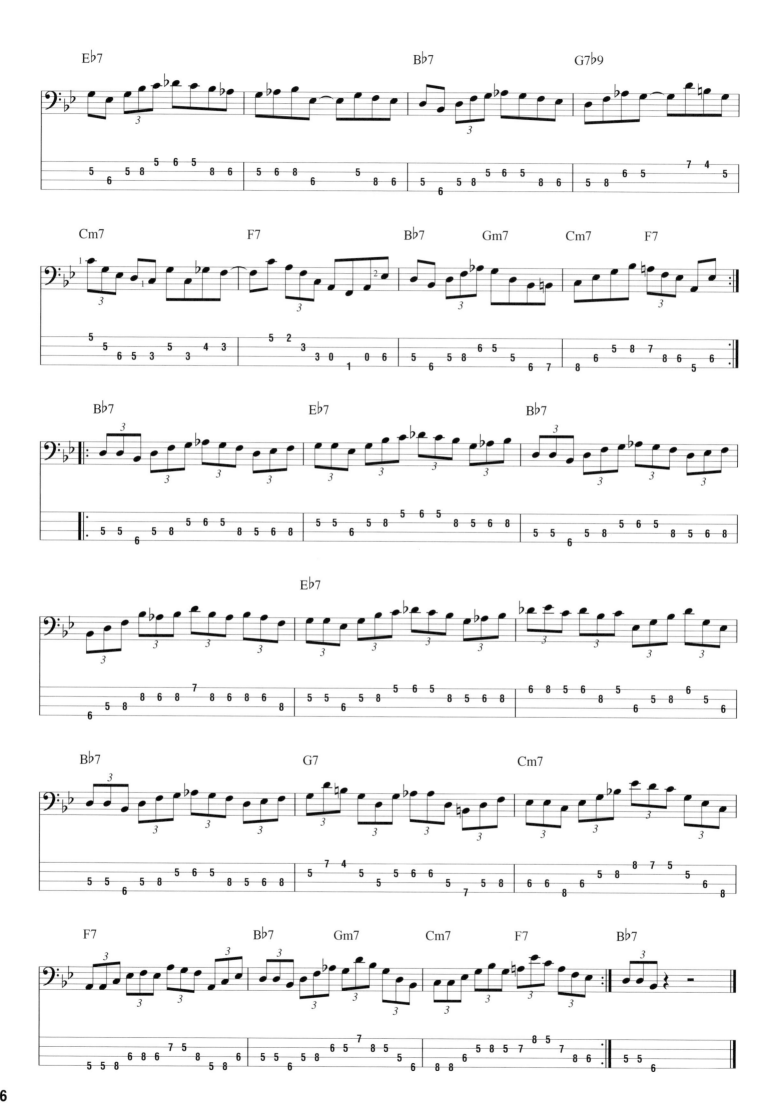

JAZZ 3

JAZZ 4

JAZZ 5

*2nd time, fret D note on
2nd string, 12th fret.

*2nd time, fret D note on 1st string, 7th fret.

JAZZ 6

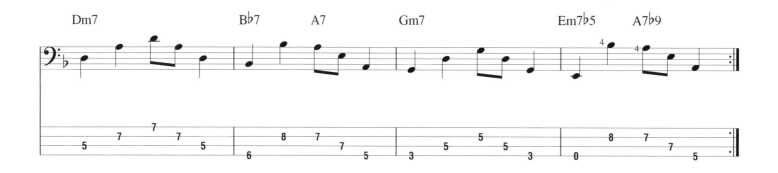

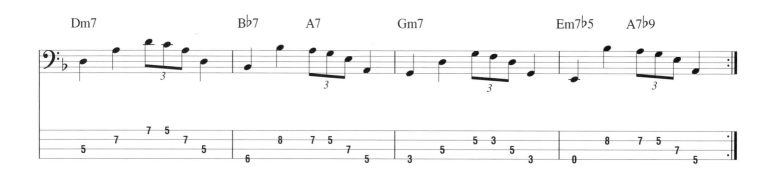

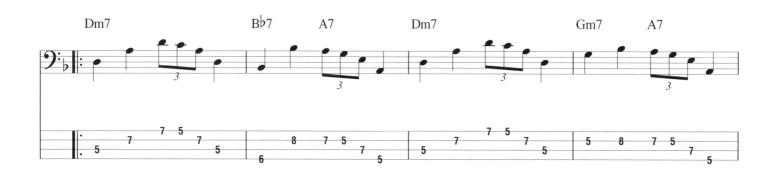

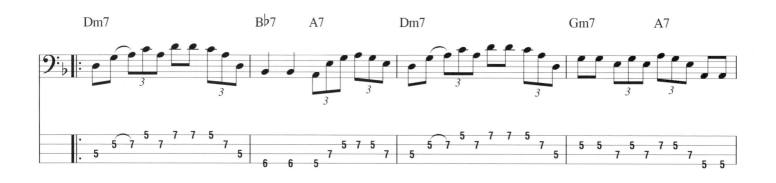

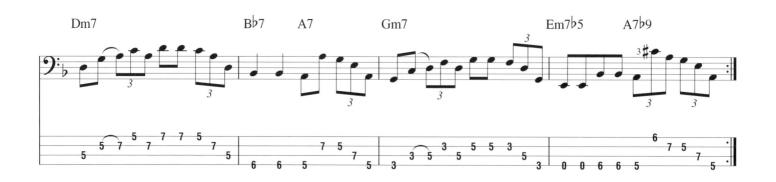

JAZZ 7

Chapter 3: Rock Chops

ROCK 1

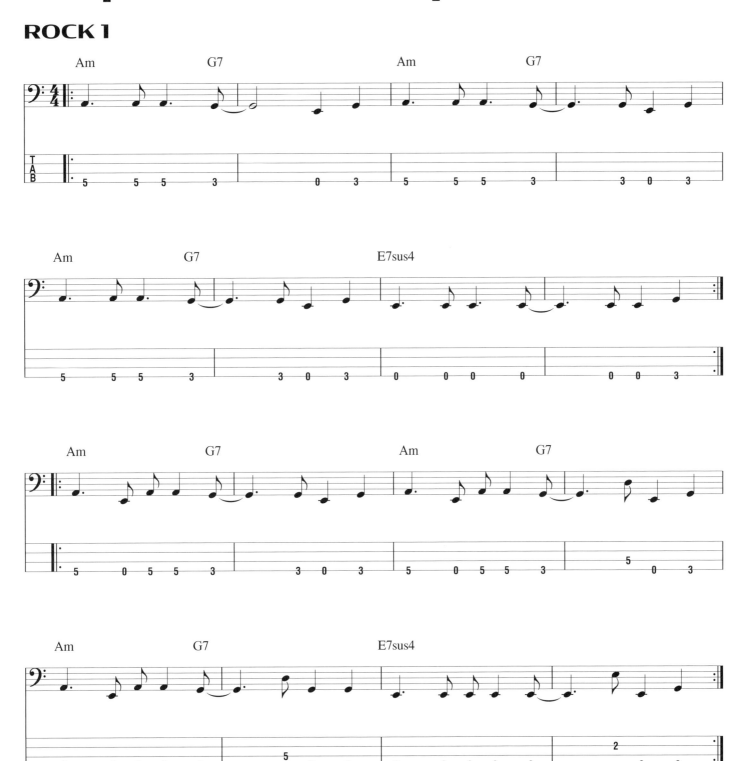

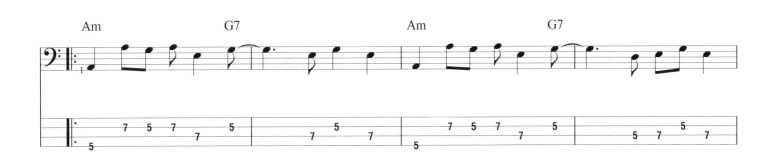

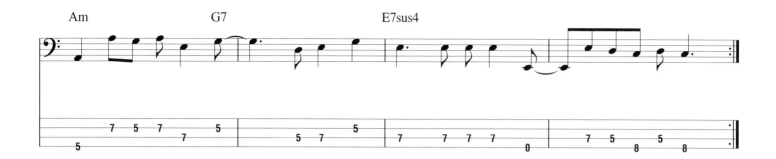

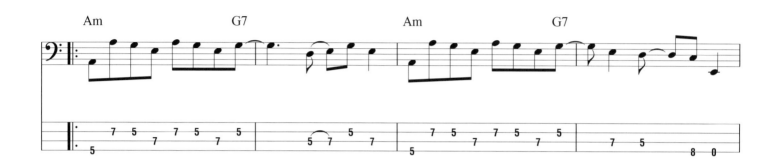

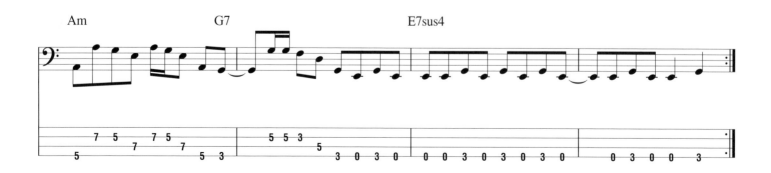

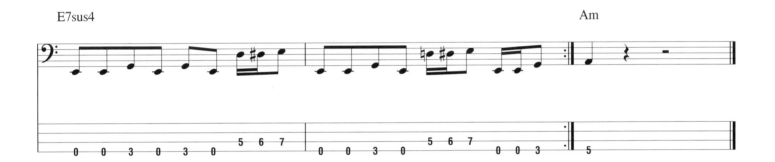

ROCK 2

ROCK 3

ROCK 4

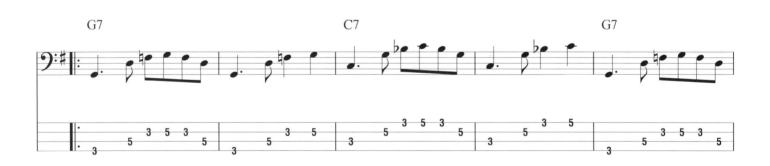

ROCK 5

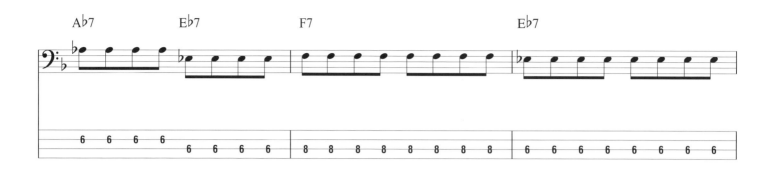

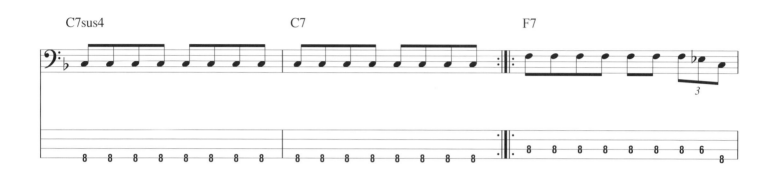

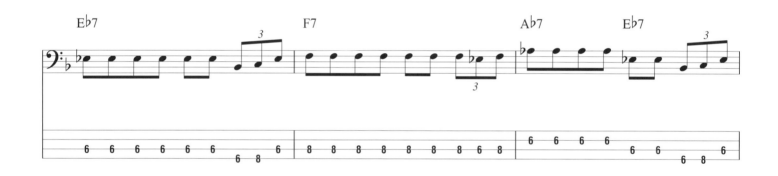

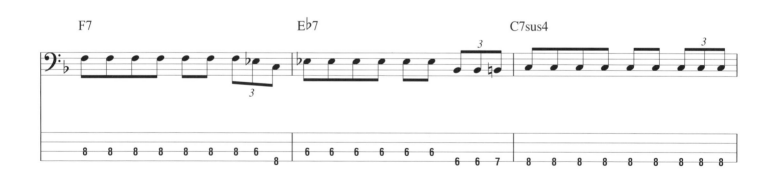

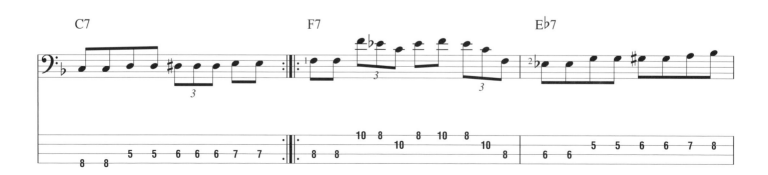

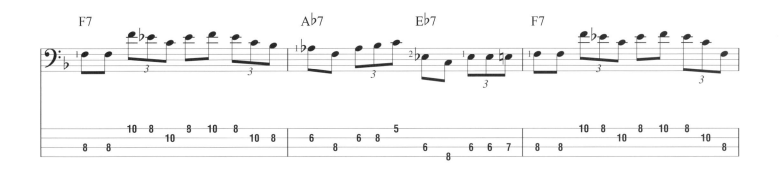

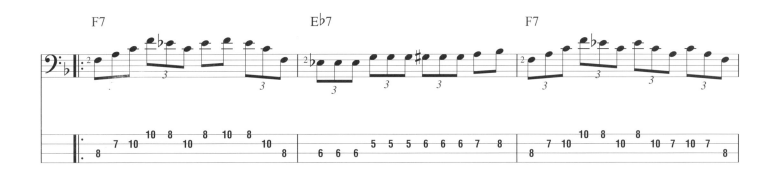

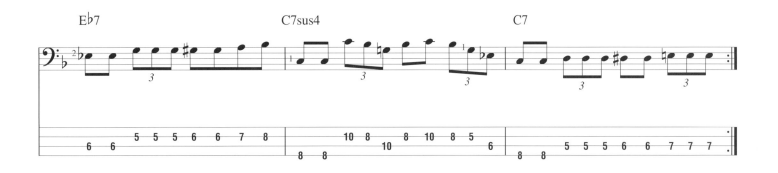

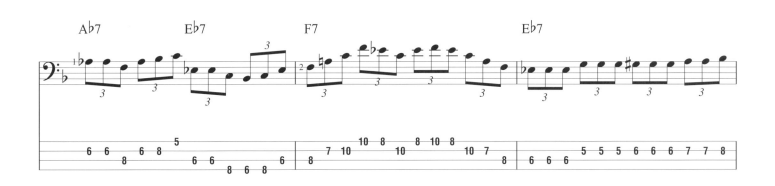

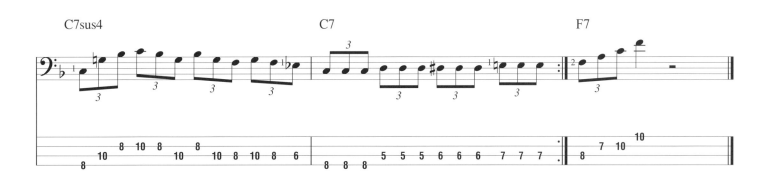

ROCK 6

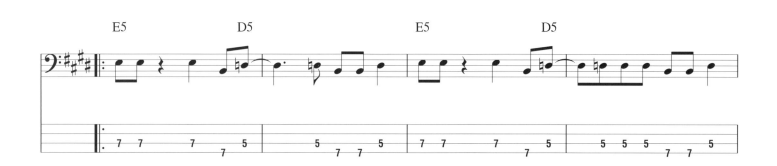

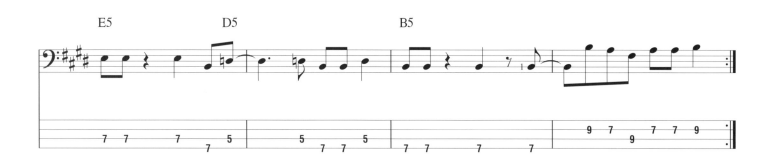

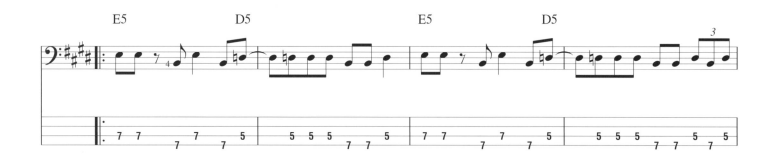

ROCK 7

ROCK 8

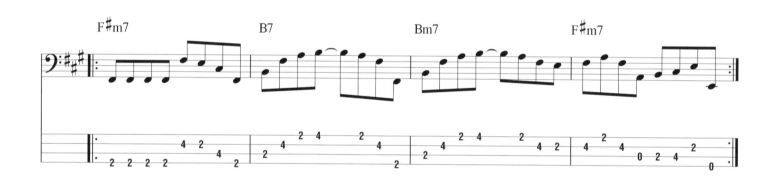

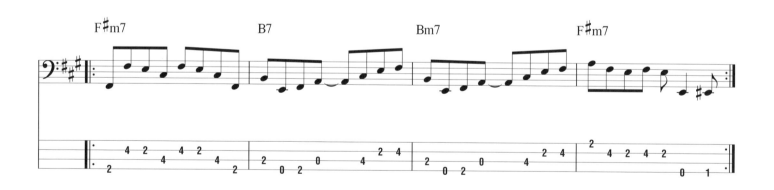

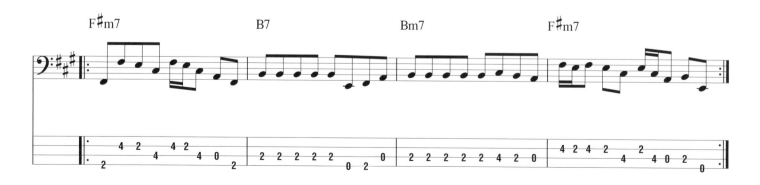

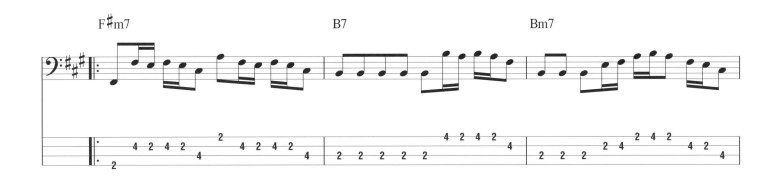

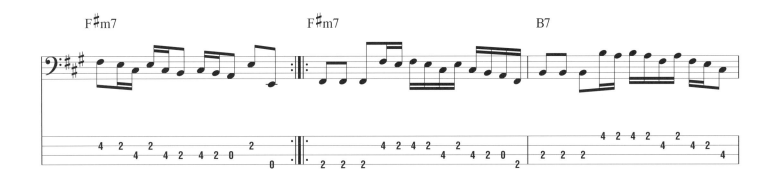

Chapter 4: Fusion Chops

FUSION 1

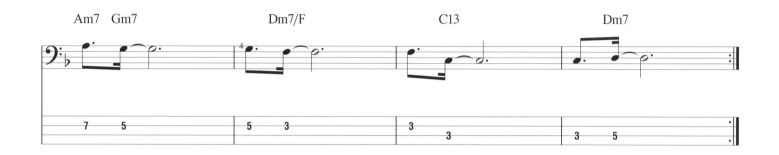

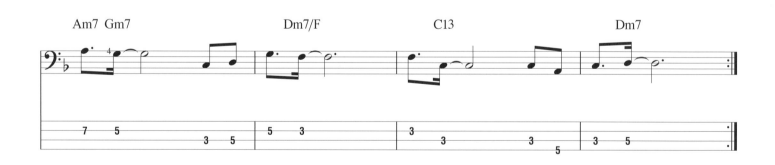

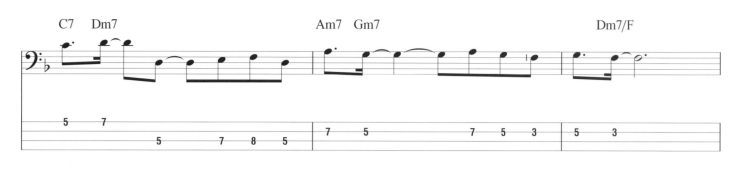

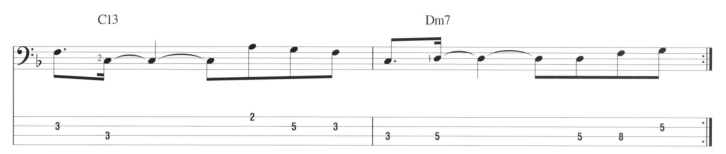

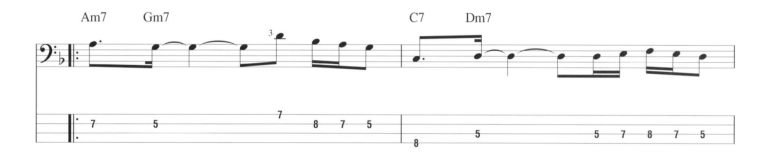

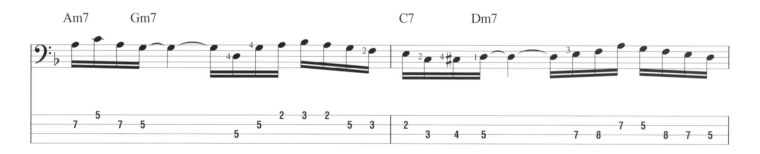

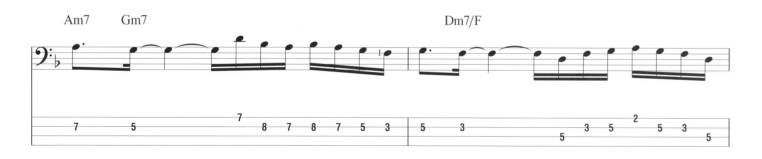

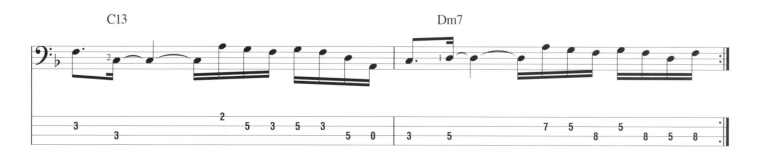

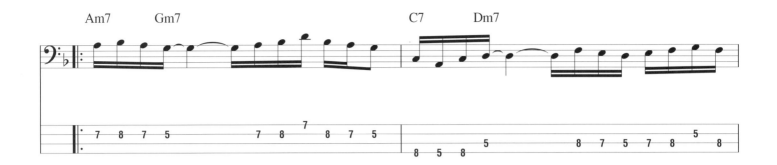

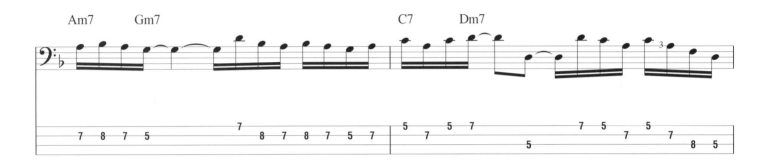

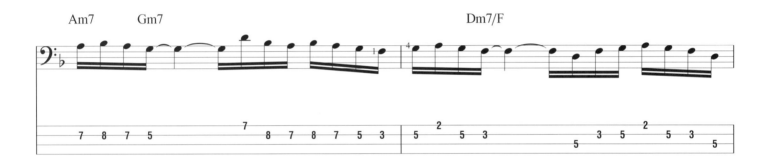

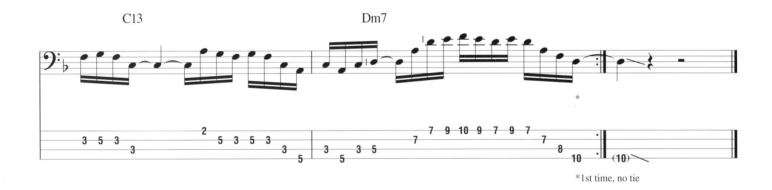

*1st time, no tie

FUSION 2

FUSION 3

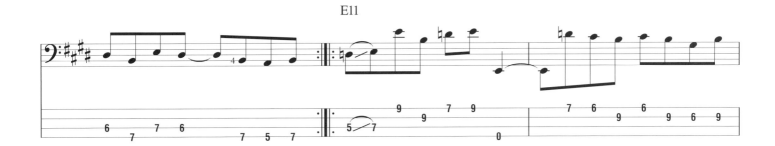

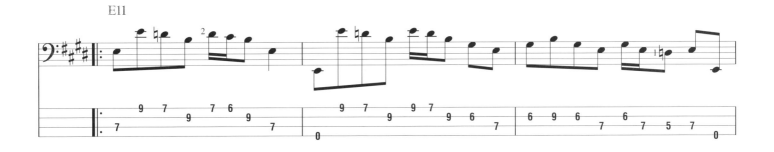

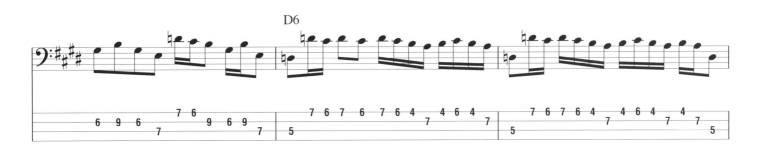

FUSION 4

FUSION 5

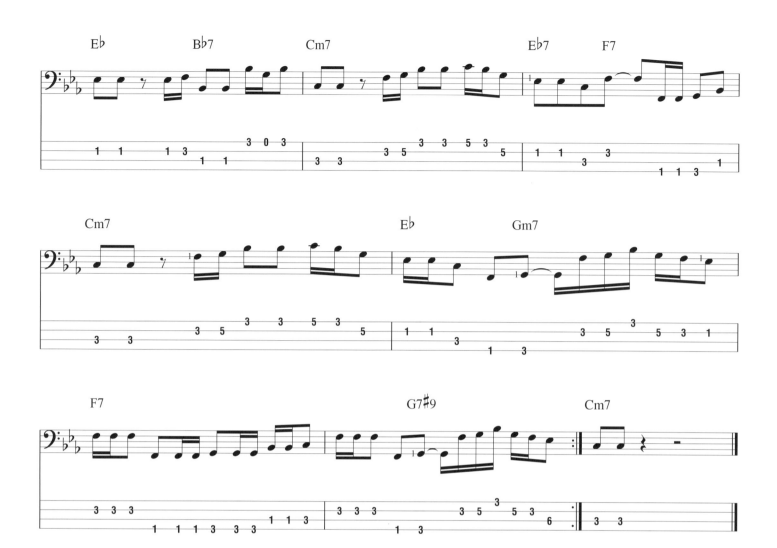

FUSION 6

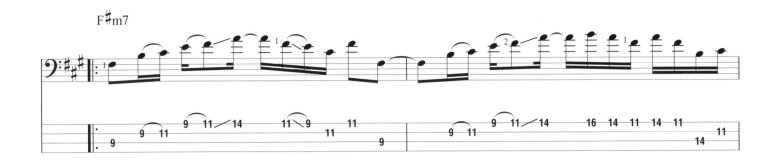

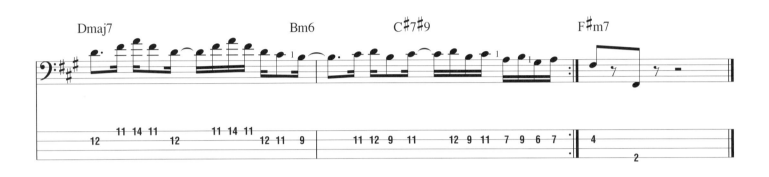

FUSION 7

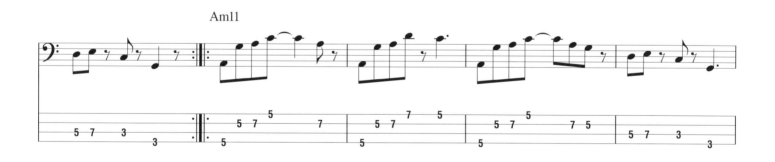

Chapter 5: R&B Chops

R&B 1

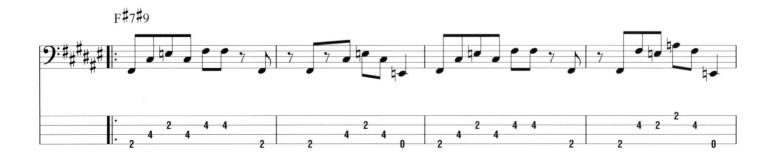

F#7#9

F#7#9

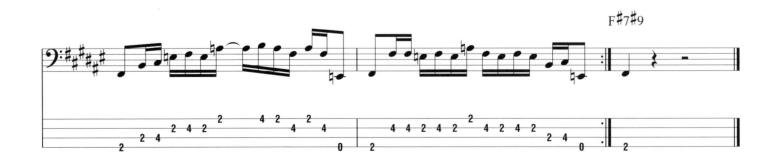

R&B 2

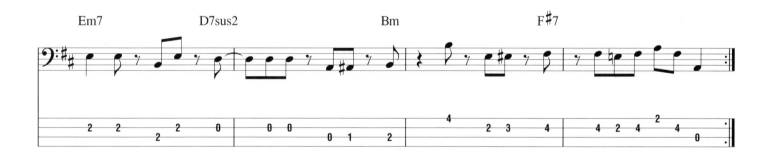

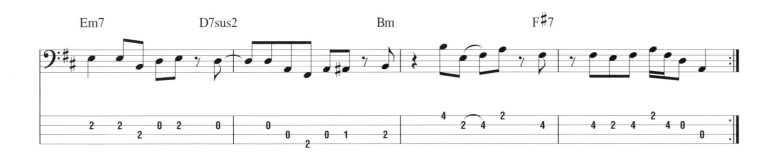

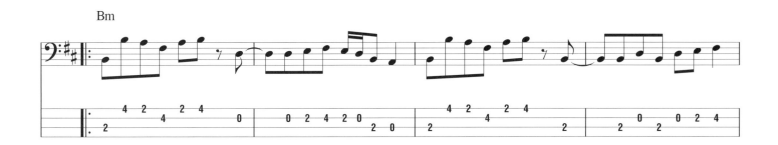

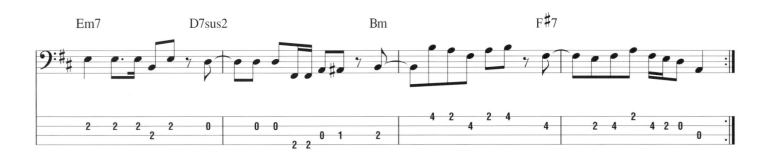

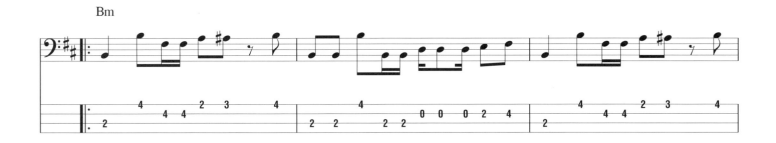

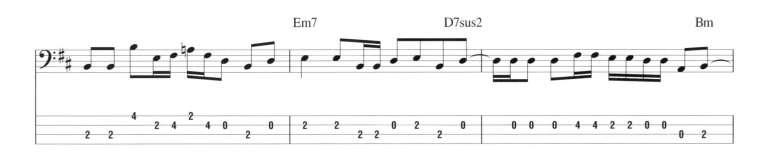

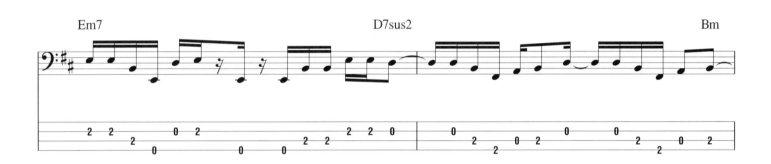

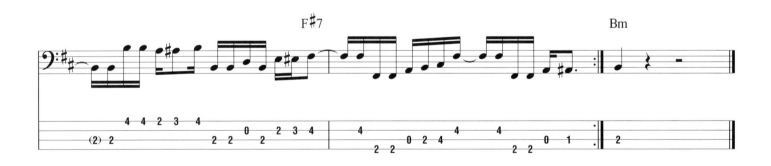

R&B 3

R&B 4

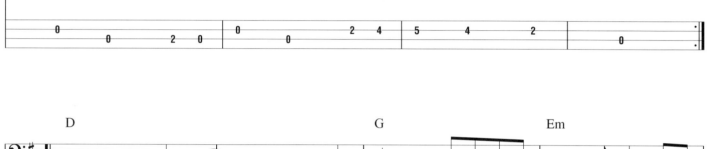

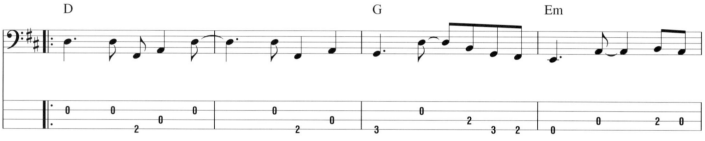

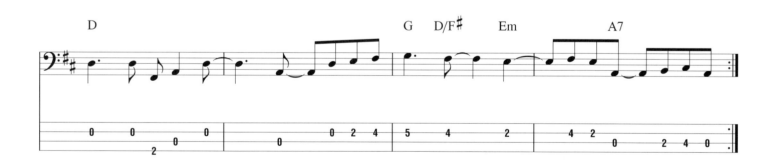

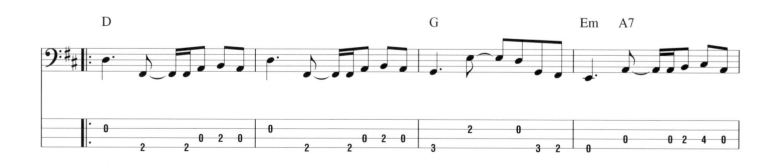

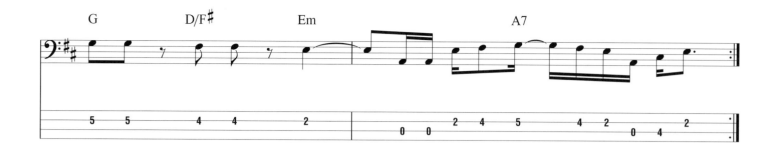

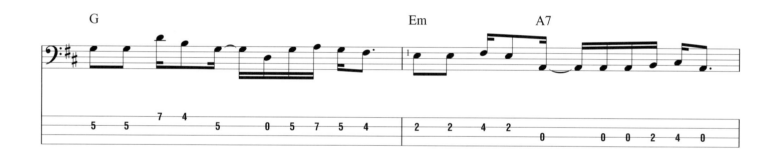

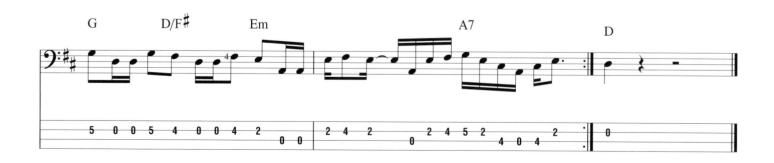

R&B 5

R&B 6

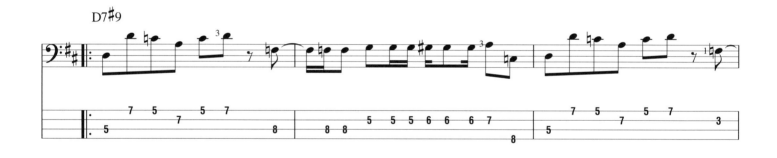

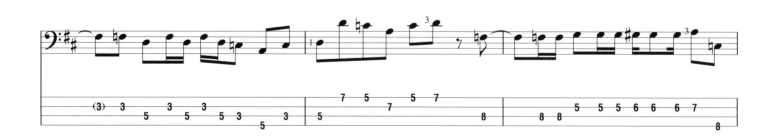

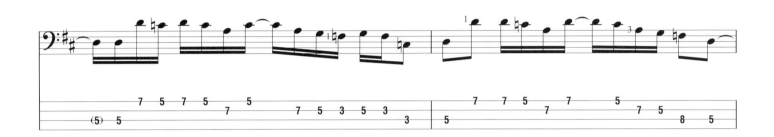

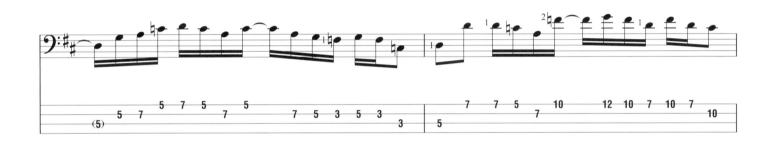

D7#9

R&B 7

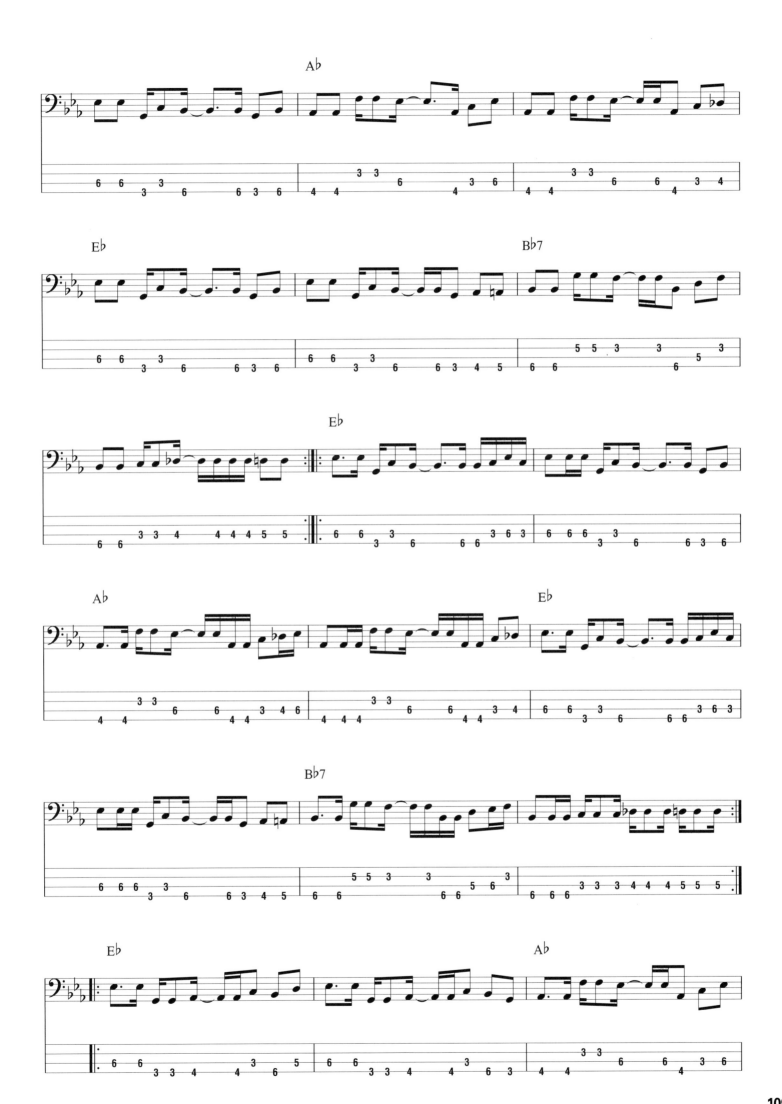

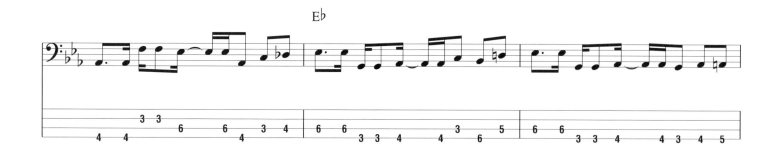

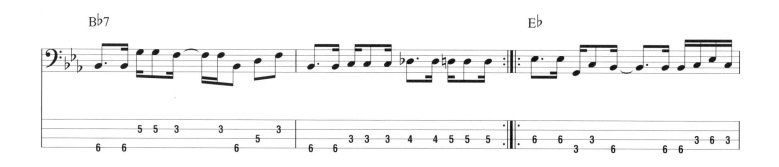

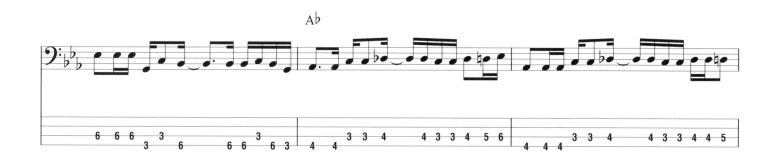

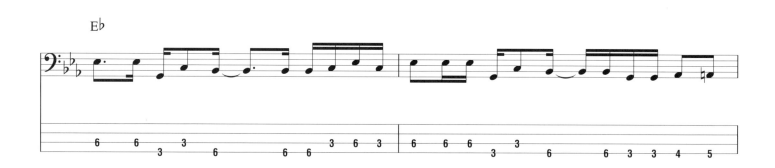

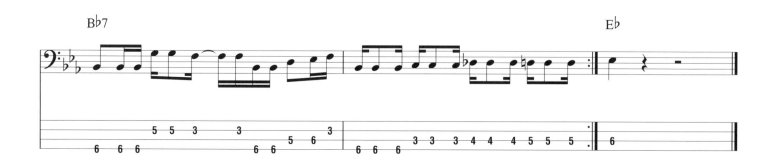

R&B 8

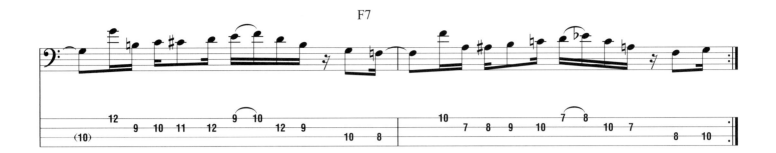

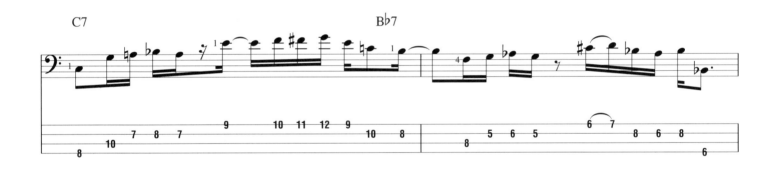

Chapter 6: Slapping Chops

SLAPPING 1

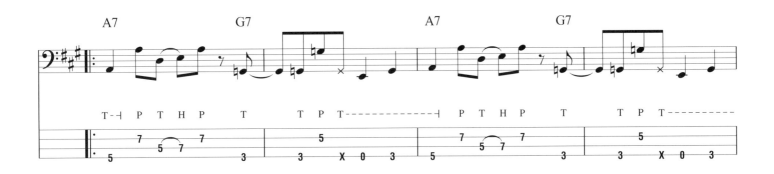

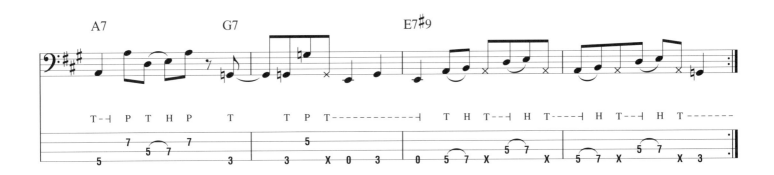

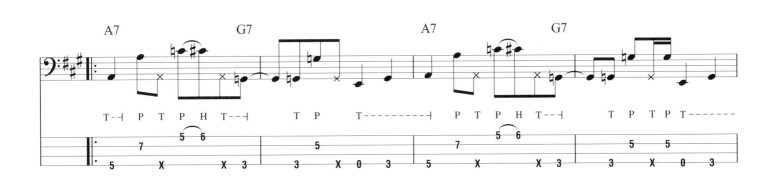

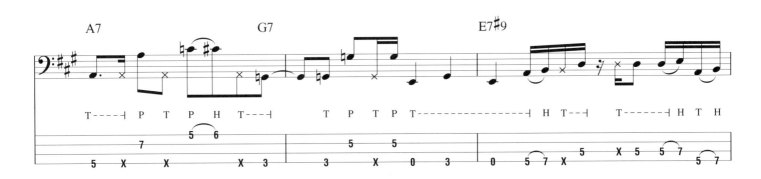

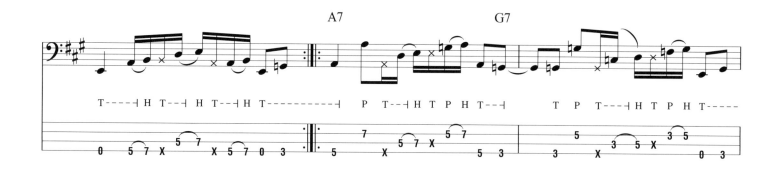

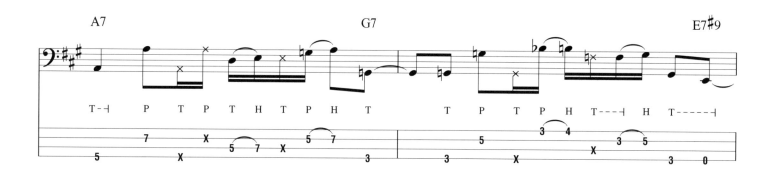

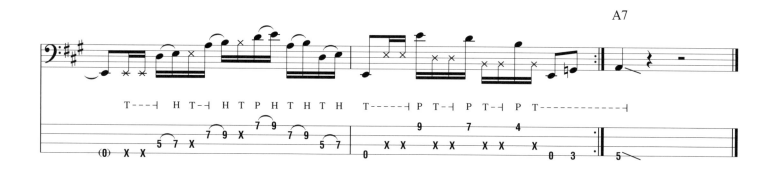

SLAPPING 2

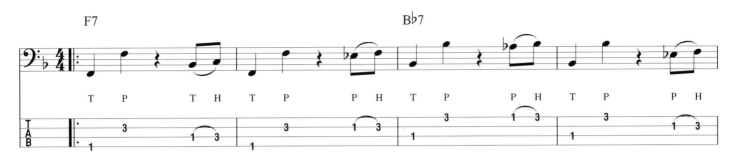

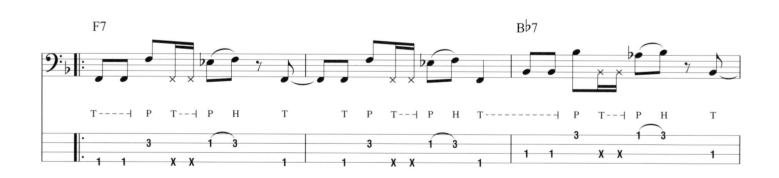

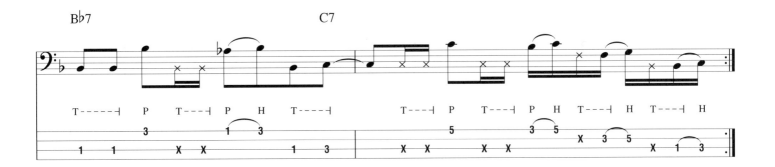

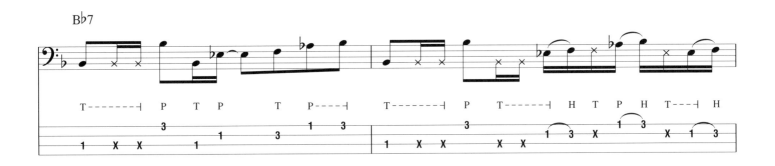

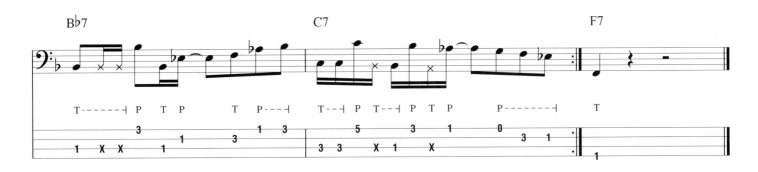

SLAPPING 3

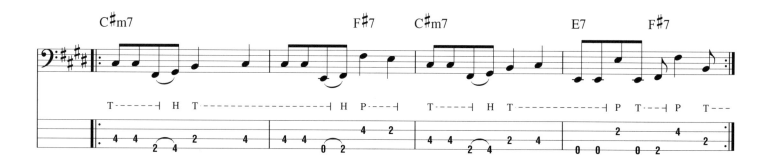

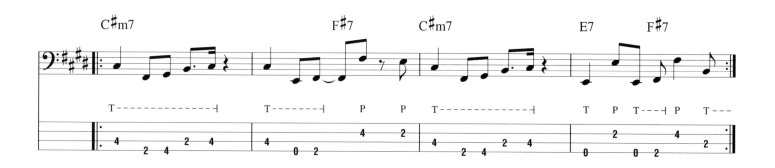

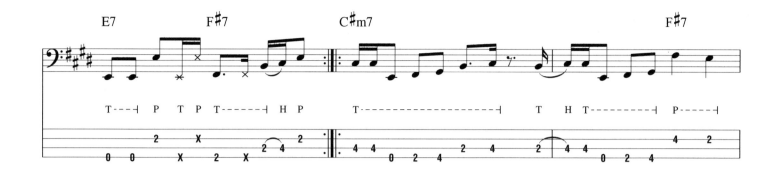

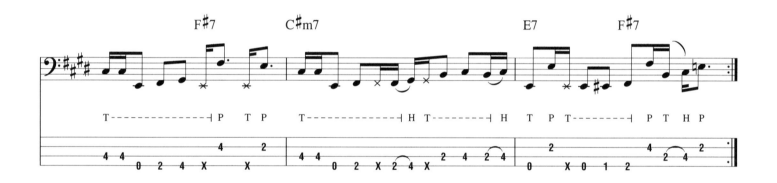

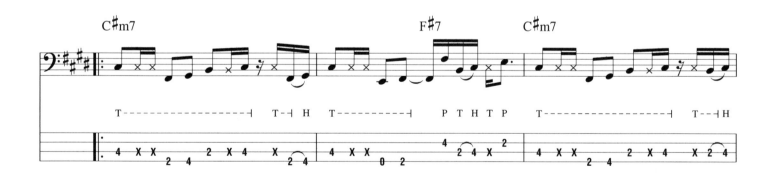

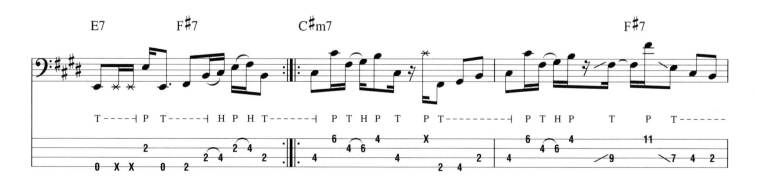

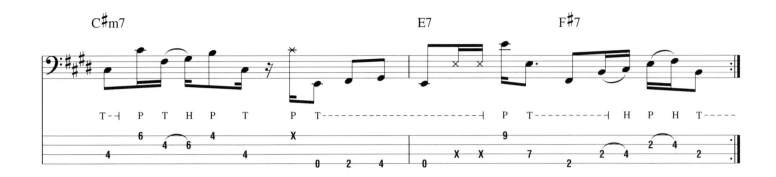

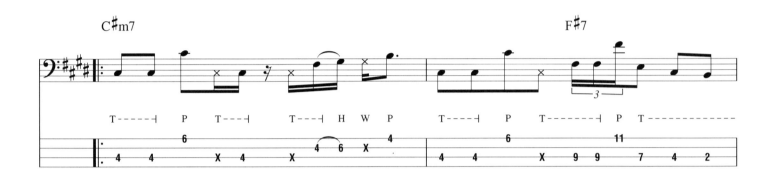

SLAPPING 4

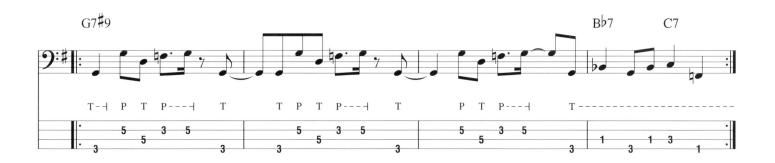

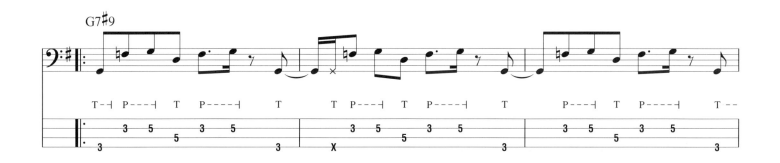

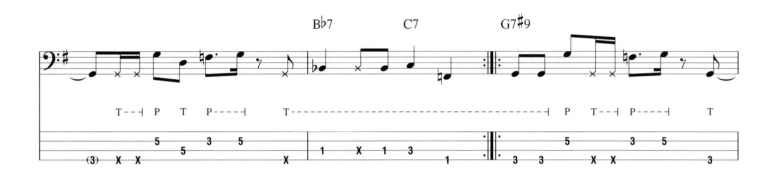

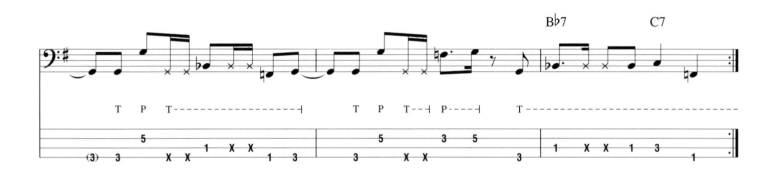

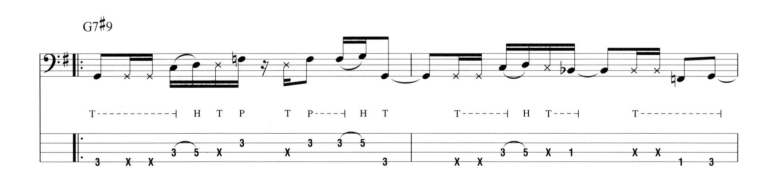

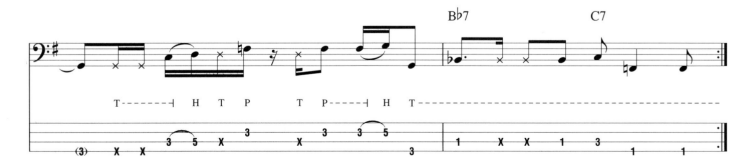

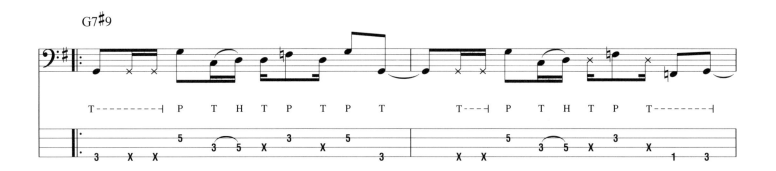

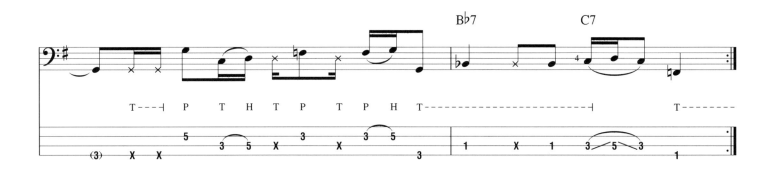

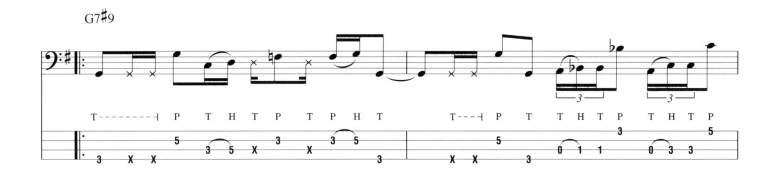

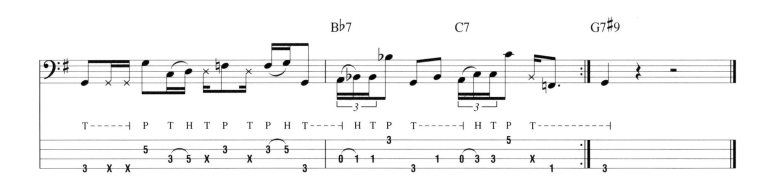

SLAPPING 5

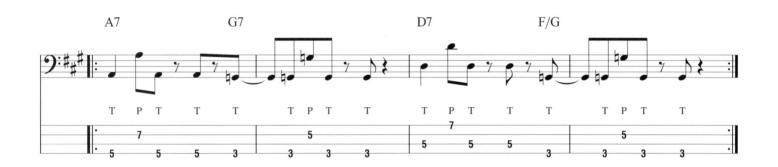

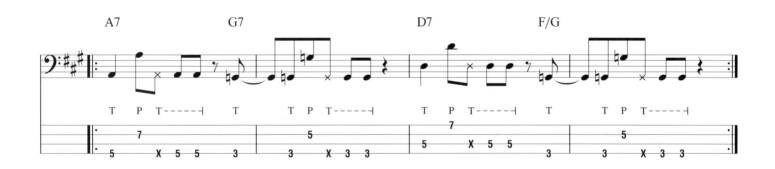

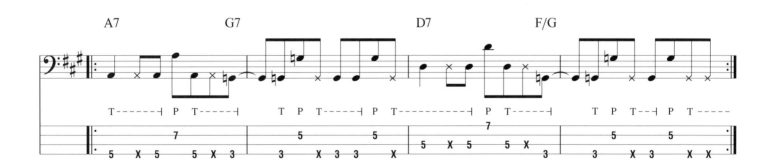

SLAPPING 6

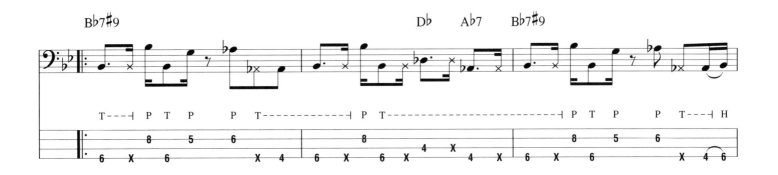

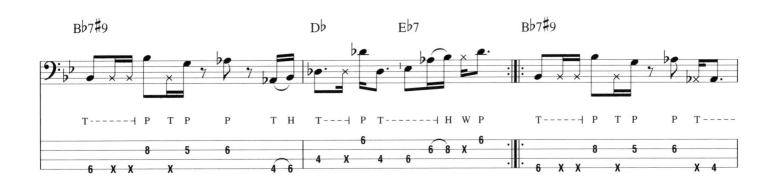

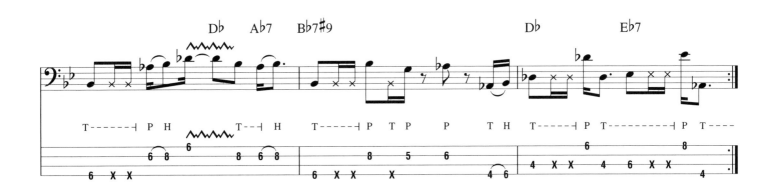

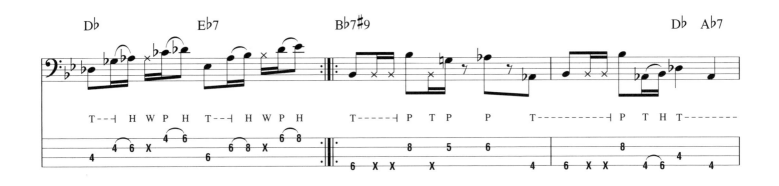

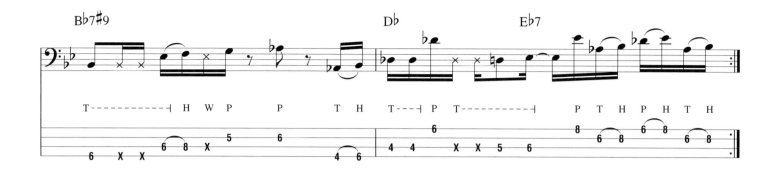

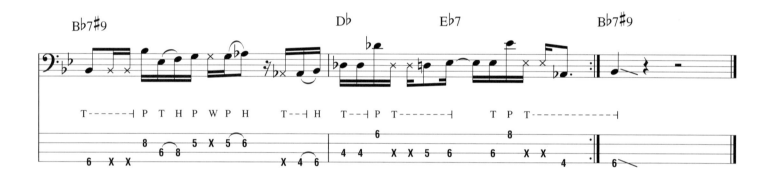

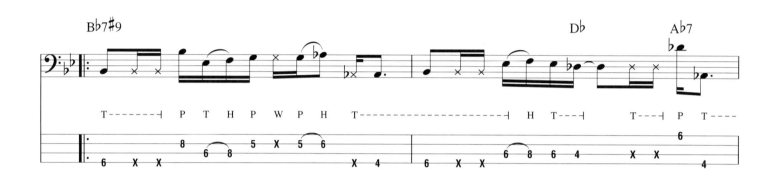

SLAPPING 7

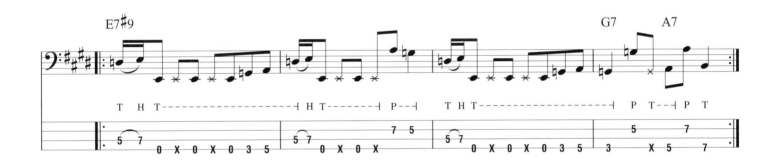

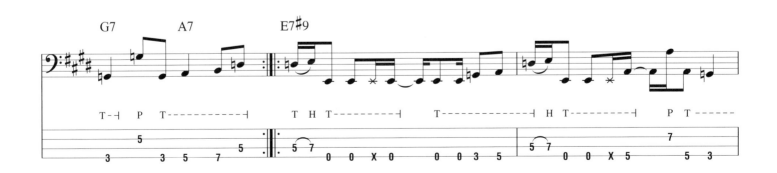

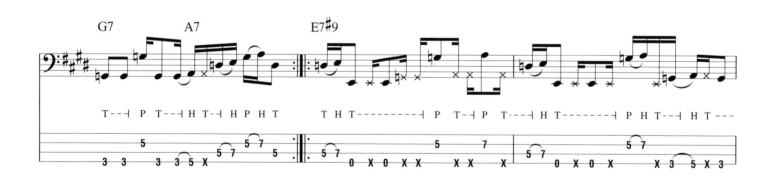

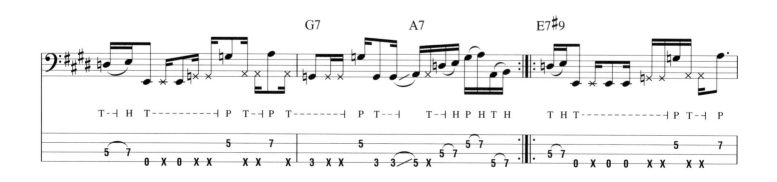

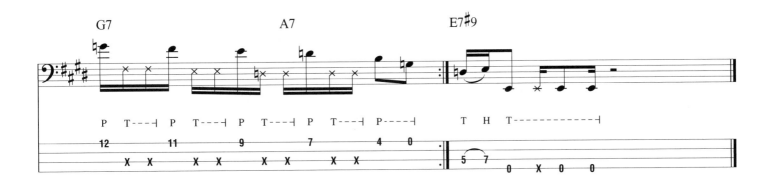

ABOUT THE AUTHOR

Jon Liebman is a world-renowned bassist, composer, arranger, author, and educator. He has played electric and acoustic bass in every imaginable setting, from jazz gigs and club dates to full-scale concerts and internationally broadcast radio and TV shows. Jon has performed in many of the world's major concert venues, including New York's Madison Square Garden, L.A.'s Shrine Auditorium, and Tokyo's spectacular Suntory Hall (not to mention bull rings in Central America, amphitheaters in the Caribbean, and all kinds of offbeat settings across the globe).

Photo by Randy Zdrojewski

Throughout the course of a career that began over 30 years ago, Jon has performed and/or toured with a wide range of musical acts, including: Amy Grant, Cleo Laine, Buddy DeFranco, Billy Eckstine, Eartha Kitt, the Drifters, the Platters, the Coasters, the Chiffons, the Ink Spots, the Fifth Dimension, Julio Iglesias, José Feliciano, Ira Sullivan, Ralphe Armstrong, Gregory Hines, Theodore Bikel, and countless others. He has performed in the pit orchestras of many Broadway shows, including *Dreamgirls*, *Ain't Misbehavin'*, *Phantom of the Opera*, *Les Misérables*, *Fiddler on the Roof*, *Oliver!*, *A Funny Thing Happened on the Way to the Forum*, *Golden Boy*, *Kiss of the Spider Woman*, *Annie*, and many others. He's also supplied bass tracks for major recording projects for clients which have included Ford, GM, and the NBA. In addition, Jon has had his big-band arrangements performed on *The Tonight Show*, *The Late Show*, and other programs.

As an educator, Jon's best-selling books and highly acclaimed online instruction series have helped hundreds of thousands of bassists improve their playing, and are part of the curricula of many music schools, colleges, and universities throughout the world. In addition to *Bass Chops*, Liebman is the author of *Funk Bass*, *Funk/Fusion Bass*, *Rock Bass*, *Blues Bass*, *Bass Grooves: The Ultimate Collection*, *Bass Aerobics*, *Play Like Jaco Pastorius: The Ultimate Bass Lesson*, and *First 15 Lessons: Bass Guitar*, as well as a book of transcriptions of the music of fellow bassist and friend Stuart Hamm. Jon also undertook the daunting task of performing all the bass tracks on Hal Leonard's newest *Jaco Pastorius Bass Play-Along*.

Jon holds a Bachelor of Music degree in Jazz Studies & Contemporary Media from Wayne State University in Detroit and a Master of Music degree in Studio Music & Jazz from the University of Miami in Coral Gables, Florida. Jon has spent time in California, where he was active in the Los Angeles music scene as a performer and writer.

As the founder of Notehead MediaGroup, LLC, Jon conceived and developed the very popular *www.ForBassPlayersOnly.com*, one of the most popular sources in the world for online bass instruction. The site also features hundreds of one-on-one interviews Jon has conducted with some of the most famous bass players in the world. Jon lives in Michigan with his wife Mindy and has four children.

BASS NOTATION LEGEND

Bass music can be notated two different ways: on a *musical staff,* and in *tablature*

THE MUSICAL STAFF shows pitches and rhythms and is divided by bar lines into measures. Pitches are named after the first seven letters of the alphabet.

TABLATURE graphically represents the bass fingerboard. Each horizontal line represents a string, and each number represents a fret.

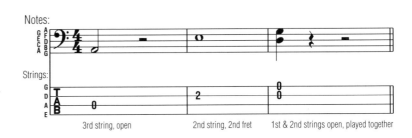

3rd string, open   2nd string, 2nd fret   1st & 2nd strings open, played together

HAMMER-ON: Strike the first (lower) note with one finger, then sound the higher note (on the same string) with another finger by fretting it without picking.

PULL-OFF: Place both fingers on the notes to be sounded. Strike the first note and without picking, pull the finger off to sound the second (lower) note.

LEGATO SLIDE: Strike the first note and then slide the same fret-hand finger up or down to the second note. The second note is not struck.

SHIFT SLIDE: Same as legato slide, except the second note is struck.

TRILL: Very rapidly alternate between the notes indicated by continuously hammering on and pulling off.

TREMOLO PICKING: The note is picked as rapidly and continuously as possible.

VIBRATO: The string is vibrated by rapidly bending and releasing the note with the fretting hand.

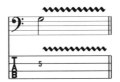

SHAKE: Using one finger, rapidly alternate between two notes on one string by sliding either a half-step above or below.

NATURAL HARMONIC: Strike the note while the fret hand lightly touches the string directly over the fret indicated.

MUFFLED STRINGS: A percussive sound is produced by laying the fret hand across the string(s) without depressing them and striking them with the pick hand.

BEND: Strike the note and bend up the interval shown.

BEND AND RELEASE: Strike the note and bend up as indicated, then release back to the original note. Only the first note is struck.

RIGHT-HAND TAP: Hammer ("tap") the fret indicated with the "pick-hand" index or middle finger and pull off to the note fretted by the fret hand.

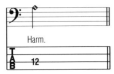

LEFT-HAND TAP: Hammer ("tap") the fret indicated with the "fret-hand" index or middle finger.

SLAP: Strike ("slap") string with right-hand thumb.

POP: Snap ("pop") string with right-hand index or middle finger.

Additional Musical Definitions

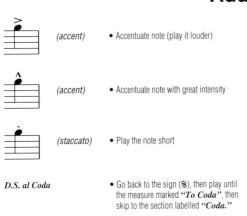

(accent) • Accentuate note (play it louder)

(accent) • Accentuate note with great intensity

(staccato) • Play the note short

D.S. al Coda • Go back to the sign (𝄋), then play until the measure marked ***"To Coda"***, then skip to the section labelled ***"Coda."***

Fill • Label used to identify a brief pattern which is to be inserted into the arrangement.

• Repeat measures between signs.

• When a repeated section has different endings, play the first ending only the first time and the second ending only the second time.

The following notation is used in the "Slapping" chapter:

T = Thumb slap

P = Pop

H = Hammer-on

X = "Dead" note

W = Strike the strings with your plucking-hand wrist